# Between the lines

Priscilla Collazo

BookLeaf
Publishing

India | USA | UK

Presentation by *BookLeaf Publishing*

Web: www.bookleafpub.com

E-mail: info@bookleafpub.com

ISBN: 9789360943639

First edition 2024

# Happy Place

It was a Monday morning
Sun was shining bright
The smell of fresh coffee brewing

My toes buried in the sand
My curls flowing in the wind
Closing my eyes, I drifted for a moment
Listening to the sound of the
waves crashing onto the shore

It was a Monday morning
Segal's were circling the sky
In search of their next meal
I watched in amazement as they
Scooped into the ocean pulling up
a mouth full of water

I sat in the sand enjoying nature in its rarest
form

It was a Monday evening
I watched the sunset
The sky changed from blue to pinks and purples
Thoughts of cotton candy

The sand started to feel cold
I was one with the earth
For a moment it was serene

This will always be my happy place

# The Last Time

The last time I saw you, your smile was bright
and your eyes were sad.

I wanted to ask but, I also wanted us to enjoy the
brightness.

The thought never crossed my mind.

The last time I saw you my heart was full, while
yours happen to be broken.

We went for a walk. Enjoying New York City,
and all it's chaos.

Not realizing chaos was brewing inside you.

The last time I saw you we took silly pictures
and exchanged embraces.

We said I love you's through laughter and tears.

The thought never crossed my mind.

The last time I saw you, you were present yet so
far. I wanted to ask but I also wanted to hear
your voice full of excitement.

The last time I saw you the day was beautiful
and warm.

Your sad eyes told a story one I wasn't ready to
hear.

The day I saw you, it was cold and dark.

You broke my heart.

The story I wasn't ready to hear was spoken.
Smiles were now frowns and tears of laughter
were tears for loss.

The last time I saw you we didn't see each other
at all.

# Late Nights

My nights have turned into moments of truths

There I was lost in a daze, thoughts running wild
awaiting to be set free, thoughts that would soon
fade and become distant memories

A free spirit is how I plan on living my life

Like a wild fire, you sparked a flame
A flame I can't seem to put out, but let's be
serious am I really even trying?

Am I allowing myself to be vulnerable with no
real intentions of giving myself to you.

Late nights, strong drinks, lusty eyes

You grab my hand and led me to the edge. I sat
between your legs and we reminisced

You traced my face with your fingers pushing
my curls out of the way

You stop at my chin, lift my head up and kiss me
softly, I linger there with my eyes closed,
secretly not wanting this moment to end

Late nights, sweet dreams and good nights

I'm at the edge debating if tonight I will accept
my truths, move pass my demons and fall into
love again…

# Moments

Some moments are meant to just be thought up
and never happen.
While other moments take over your life.
Smiles, frowns, crying faces all do one thing
show emotion.

If I tell you what I'm thinking will you still love
me?
If I give up will I love me?

Moments are best when you share them with
someone but sometimes moments are just that a
glimpse of something unreal.

The desire of the unknown all while living in a
moment.

# Sunny

Sun kissed skin.
Hair blowing in the wind.
Blue skies.
Big waves.
Random thoughts...

Beach days are the best days to unwind and day
dream.
I dreamt of you today while the waves crashed
against the sand.

Remembering that night on the beach where it
felt like it was just you and I.
Kisses we shared while sitting at the life guards
chair.

Now the Sun is setting and so are my day
dreams.

# Valentine

In the mist of all the things happening in the world, I took a moment to love myself.

To love another person.
To tell the ones you care for, I LOVE YOU.
To take a breath.
To enjoy a moment that last more than 24 hours.

To stop.

We have 365 days to do all these things but 2/14 always seems like the day where people allow themselves to be vulnerable.

We have it all wrong.

Valentine's Day is a day that makes you stop and smell the roses. A day to make show the most effort. To realize that you haven't had date night and on this day you will make it extra special.

To love the person you've been loving 364 days a little harder. The one day all else is put to rest, while they get dressed and ready to be appreciated.

To ask your forever Valentine to STOP and slow dance while that R&B record plays.

Valentine Days can be any day you choose, to slow down and enjoy each other.

Happy Valentine's Day, 364 plus one times.

# Summer

11

Laying on the beach with you by my side.

Soft touch, out lining my figure with your pointer finger.

Sun kissed and kisses from you is all I need.

As I play with the sand I draw hearts because I love where I am.

Water waves and splashing around, creating memories with you.

Don't look into my eyes, you will lose yourself in my stories.

# Change

Life has many paths and within those paths, you find a new version of yourself.

In those paths you may not find the same friends and that's ok, because it means they have served their purpose and they weren't meant to be a part of the next chapter.

Within this paths, lovers will become distant memories, good and bad. You will learn what you like and what you are willing to settle for. What you are willing to accept and what you want to leave behind. You will gain new experiences that you can take with you, on your next journey.

Change can be whatever you make it.

Change for me is growth.

It has been a bitter sweet journey. I have partied, like it was my last night on this beautiful planet. I have loved is hard, I put him on a pedestal and down he fell. I have called friends crying and with tears came laughter. I have traveled, laid nude on the beach, basking in the sun. Oh how I love summer. I have felt lost and alone, in a room full of people. I have emailed all while feeling broken. I had forgotten what it felt like to live life.

Until that day...

The day I started to feel alive.
A new path, a new journey.
I named this particular journey, she just needed a name. I called her ME.

I held my head up high and I was able to smile, genuinely. Putting ME first felt different almost wrong. But with these changes, what's meant to be will be. The friends and family that will join ME on this journey, are welcome to the changes within ME.

To see ME grow
To see ME live
To see ME become
To see ME thrive in Change.

# I AM

My parents daughter.

Hello Mother, can you tell me the story of how I became to be.

The short version, two people came together, one with experience and the other a virgin. In-love and blinded, we made love and two weeks later I found out I was pregnant.

Hello Father, can you tell me the story of how I become to be.
Confused by the question, it took him a second to gather his thoughts and finally he said…

The short version, We both were young and in-love. The moment was one that we both wanted. The love was real and we were blinded by it.

I was created with love in the heart.

I am a lover girl at heart and they are the reason why.

My heart has broken over and over again but
with each break it mended to be loved again.

Imperfect and still I am able to love hard.

I am strong, my love is resilient.

I wear my heart on my sleeve and I allow my
heart to lead.

Leading me through hurdles in darkness and
blinding me by bright colors.

I am the one you love.

I am my parents daughter.

# Secret Lover

Meet me at the place around 8pm
We will have drinks and chat about nothing, and
every thing

Meet me at that place around you know the one
with the good food and sangria

Let us dive into memory lane and stroll pass
good times all while cheering to the future and
secrets

Oh hey there lover, let's get lost in the dark and
kiss under trees while rain drops fall around us

Meet at the spot that makes us laugh and cry,
you know the place.

Secret lover

Meet me between the sheets, where we lay
intertwined and tell stories about life.

A secret is kept because why let the world
disturb, adventure

Meet me at the place with the sparkly lights,
where excitement awaits and danger is explored
and stories are told, over and over again.

# A beautiful Read

What a beautiful day to sit under a willow tree and read

Reading a novel about two strangers who fall in love

My eyes will fill with tears of joy

I am in love with being in love, a true lover girl

I take a moment to take in the story as the warm breeze blows through my curls

I close my eyes and the tears fall I can smell the freshness of spring

I wipe my tears and take a deep breath. I watch as the willow sways, back and forth almost covering me. For a second I am invincible to the world.

What a beautiful day to escape reality and fall into a mystery, one that keeps the pages turning and your eyes wide with excitement, you get to the end and gasp. It was truly unexpected. You

were truly unexpected, a stranger who became a
true life dream, but still a mystery.

The joy of a new book

Some people enjoy the smell of a new car but
place me in a book store and the smell of love,
mystery, danger, history, is all too good to miss.

What a beautiful day to get lost in a book.

# Blinded

It was those moments when everything around you froze and it was just you and your thoughts.

You would think of the way they walked, talked, and the way they placed their hand in yours, making you feel safe.

You would speak of them in the highest regard.

They were PERFECT.

It was in those moments when the world was still and you would smile to yourself, believing that you couldn't be any happier. That this person was your person and how incredibly lucky you are.

No one could have told you different and no one bothered too.

Its those precious moments that blind you, into believing you are in-love.

Rose colored glasses start to fade and perfections aren't so pretty.

You want to believe that this person is your
person but how?

When you feel tricked.

Blinded by their charm
Blinded by their good looks
Blinded by their efforts
Blinded by their lies

The touch of the hand doesn't feel safe, but
strange. A stranger playing to your weakness, to
your wanting to be loved.

# Afraid

A little nervous
A little afraid

The thought of us not being able to
we are two young, gentle souls, enjoying life
and it's possibilities

Why all the worry, why all the chaos

A little nervous, that this not what we want
A little afraid of it being real

You had me who the music played and the rosé
touched our lips. We sat across from each other
and unknowingly was falling.

Falling into a love that will scare us
A love we both knew we deserved and wanted

Our hands touched

We saw a glimpse of future days

Here we sit nervous and afraid

You alone in a room full of hope
Me in a room waiting, with thoughts of laughter
and cries that could fill a quiet room

Here we sit together

Holding hands, fingers intertwined, gazing into
each others eyes

We want this, we want it with one another

A little nervous
A little afraid

# Art

The blood that runs through me is with pain and
a dash of unbelievable beauty

She came to me in a dream

I grabbed my paint brush and allowed the
creativity to take over

She was pleasure
She was desire
She was the pain my body ached for

Every stroke grew more Intense

I didn't know what would come of this madness
but I knew I needed to let it out

The dream was dark, flashes of red out lined her
body, hair long flowing in the wind

She was mesmerizing
She had a hold on me
She was my downfall

I started to take control and the strokes started to
feel lighter
was I finished
was this my master piece
was this the end of something beautiful

The blood that runs within me filled with pain

I hate it
This is worthless
People love it

Seeing the beauty in the pain

# Coffee Shop

Take me on a date
No expectations
Comfy clothes and a messy bun

Let's go on a date
Hot latte and ice coffee
Bonding over our drinks and macaroons

Morning, noon and evening, let's go on a date
In search of a story
Grinding coffee beans, filling the place with
sweet aromas

Silently sitting
Journal in hand, silver and pretty with the words
"Beauty beyond perfection" engraved

Lost in the pages as life unfolds

A sip of my coffee, fresh and delightful

Experiencing the joy of a beautiful coffee shop

Let's go on a date
Meet me in front of Steven's cafe

# Between The Lines

27

Between the lines there is always a story

A story someone told but didn't want it to be
known

Secrets

Untold

Between the lines they stood

Hidden within words

A story to be told

everyone has a different interpretation but the
story in between the lines

tells no lies

# The Beginning

My innocence was taken from me
The result was using sex as freedom

The part where you get to loose yourself in
pleasure

The satisfaction you get from see the other
person enjoy themselves

Imagination

Waiting for you to beg for it

Playing hard to get just to get what I want

It started with a forbidden kiss, one that was
taken from me

Now it's the thrill of being pinned down while
my mouth is saying not yet but my body is
saying yes

It's the part of not knowing who I am but
knowing how it started

The innocence
The silence
The getting caught
The punishment
The desire for more

The beginning lead me here

# Songs

Remember the days when songs would set the mood.

The songs that made you feel grown and sexy and ready for the night.

You would Put that one song on that made you think of that special someone, without having a special someone.

The songs that made you wish that you missed someone so much you can dedicate the song to them.

Remember the songs that made you think you were so in-love when you were really lusting over someone.

All we had was our imagination.

We put the one song on that made us dance in front of the mirror.

A space where we were able to be ourselves. We admired the way our hips, you would place your

hands around your waist and imagine someone
admiring your moves. The music would take
over and we would get lost in the beat.

That song you had no business putting on replay.

Remember the part of the songs that made you
feel things you didn't understand.

Remember the tears that fell on to virgin sheets

Remembering the songs...

# Flower

One peddle at a time until I blossomed into
something beautiful.

I was able to feed the soul, while the nectar
dripped from full lips

I was picked from all the rest

To be watered

To be exposed

On display I stood

Trying not to wither

The sun burned while the cool breeze cooled me

pieces of me hit the floor all the while there
were new versions of me

once a lonely flower

Now a bouquet full of colors

To be admired
To be held
To be given away

One peddle at a time

# Just Friends

I've always had feelings for you.
Feelings that you were unaware of.
I kept it a secret.

A secret that was burning to be told. You would
walk pass me and your beautiful curly hair
would flow in the wind. You were everything I
wanted and more. Smart, beautiful, funny and
admirable.

How could someone like you want to be with a
nerd like me?

I've always thought about kissing you under the
moon light and you falling deep in lust with me.
To hold you close and look into your eyes. To
place my hands on your face, to press my lips
against yours and create passion, is all I ever
wanted.

How do I tell you?
How do I let this secret become reality?

It just happened one day in the rain. We both
were leaving work rushing to our cars, when I
got the courage to ask you to come with me.

My heart aching for your gentle touch. Will you
want me as much as I want you?
You held my hand and squeezed tight. Was this a
sign?

I pulled you in and there we were looking into
each others eyes. It was in that moment that we
were no longer, just friends. We embrace each
other without a spoken word. I place my hand
under your chin, lifting your head up so I can
kiss you. Our tongues intertwine and our hands
gracefully explore the others body. The rain
continues to fall and every drop was euphoric.

Between both our cars we were lost in our own
magical world.

You threw your head back and I began to kiss
your neck down to your collar bone. Running
my fingers through your wet hair grasping the
back of your head. I was excited and nervous
that, this was my imagination.

I Kept my eyes closed and continued to dream.

I listened to your body, inviting me to be more
than just friends.

# Alone At Last

It's time to draw my bath after a long hard day.

I have one of those big bathtubs for two but
tonight, it's just me.
Light some candles, throw in some rose peddles
and a bath bomb, a purple one.

I go into the kitchen, while the tub is filling up
and I pour myself a glass of moscato, the sweet
kind.

I have the bottle in one hand and my glass in the
other.

I walk into the bathroom where the mirrors are
starting to fog up.
I put on my playlist a smooth jazz kind of night
and I start to gracefully move my body.

I start to slowly unbutton my shirt, unzip my
skirt and let them fall to the floor.
I stand there naked, admiring my perfect
imperfections.

I graze my hand on my breast down to my belly
button, across my hips and down my thigh and I
blow myself a kiss.

I walk toward the bath and I start to put my left
leg in, then my right.
I immerse my whole body into this warm
colorful water.
I take sip of my wine and I close my eyes.

It's time for me to unwind.